The Boston Tea Party

CORNERSTONES OF FREEDOM

SECOND SERIES

Trudi Strain Trueit

Children's Press®
A Division of Scholastic Inc.
New York • Toronto • London • Auckland • Sydney
Mexico City • New Delhi • Hong Kong
Danbury, Connecticut

Photographs © 2005: American Antiquarian Society: 38; Bridgeman
Art Library International Ltd., London/New York: 40 (John Singleton
Copley/Yale Center for British Art/Paul Mellon Collection, USA), cover
top (Library of Congress), cover bottom, 29 (Private Collection), 5
(Allan Ramsay/Private Collection), 22 (Edward Truman/Massachusetts
Historical Society, Boston, MA, USA); Corbis Images: 7, 13, 20, 27,
41, 44 right, 45 right (Bettmann), 32 (PoodlesRock), 30 (Brian Snyder/
Reuters), 3, 14; Getty Images: 11, 37 (Hulton Archive), 34 (MPI/
Hulton Archive); Mary Evans Picture Library: 35; North Wind Picture
Archives: 10, 12, 15, 16, 18, 19, 21, 24, 25, 28, 33, 45 left; Stock
Montage, Inc.: 6, 8, 44 left; Courtesy of The Bostonian Society/Old
State House: 4, 26, 36.

Library of Congress Cataloging-in-Publication Data
Trueit, Trudi Strain.
  The Boston Tea Party / Trudi Strain Trueit.
    p. cm. — (Cornerstones of freedom. Second series)
  Includes bibliographical references and index.
  ISBN 0-516-23636-9
  1. Boston Tea Party, 1773– —Juvenile literature. I. Title. II. Series.
  E215.7.T78 2005
  973.3'115—dc22   2004030162

CHILDREN'S PRESS, and CORNERSTONES OF FREEDOM™, and
associated logos are trademarks and/or registered trademarks of
Scholastic Library Publishing. SCHOLASTIC and associated logos
are trademarks and/or registered trademarks of Scholastic Inc.

1 2 3 4 5 6 7 8 9 10 R 14 13 12 11 10 09 08 07 06 05

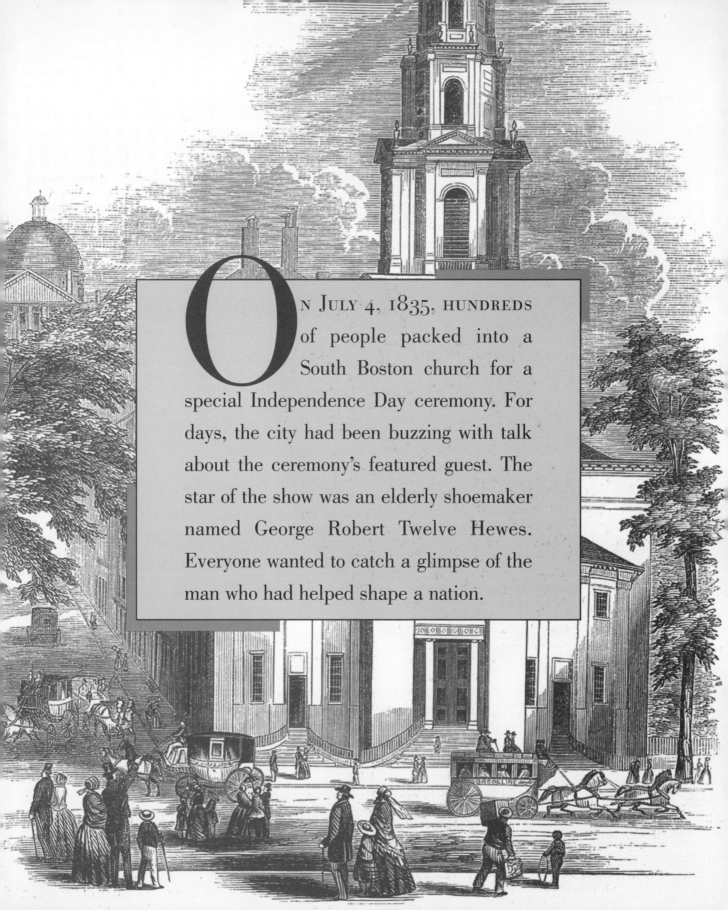

On July 4, 1835, hundreds of people packed into a South Boston church for a special Independence Day ceremony. For days, the city had been buzzing with talk about the ceremony's featured guest. The star of the show was an elderly shoemaker named George Robert Twelve Hewes. Everyone wanted to catch a glimpse of the man who had helped shape a nation.

George Robert Twelve Hewes was ninety-three-years old when Joseph G. Cole painted this portrait.

As Hewes made his way into the church, the crowd fell silent. Although he was only a little more than 5 feet (152 centimeters) tall, the old man stood straight and proud. His light brown hair had just a touch of gray, making him look far younger than his ninety-three years. As he passed, women smiled. Men removed their hats out of respect. In the last decade of his life, George Hewes had become an American hero.

In truth, Hewes was just an average citizen. Sixty-two years earlier, like thousands of other colonists, the young shoemaker was concerned about the fate of his country. On the night of December 16, 1773, he'd simply done what he felt was right. Yet, at that moment, an ordinary citizen became part of an extraordinary event. Now, in 1835, Hewes was a living symbol of liberty.

Hewes took his seat at the front of the church for the Fourth of July celebration. Before the ceremony was over, the audience would rise in thunderous applause. It was all

* * * *

to honor George Robert Twelve Hewes, one of the last surviving members of the Boston Tea Party.

A TAXING ISSUE

In 1763, Britain's King George III should have been celebrating. His troops, along with colonial **militia** and several Native American tribes, had beaten France and their Native American **allies** in the French and Indian War. Britain now controlled more than half of the North American continent. But success had come at a high price. The nation was in serious financial debt. It seemed reasonable to King George that the British colonies in America should pay their share of the war expenses. The colonies would also have to help cover the costs of continuing to defend the New World.

King George III ruled Great Britain from 1760 to 1820.

To raise funds, **Parliament** decided to **tax** its colonies. In 1764, Parliament passed the American Revenue Act, also known as the Sugar Act. The measure taxed some items brought into America from other countries, such as

5

Colonists were outraged to learn they would have to pay taxes on items from other countries.

wine, coffee, and cloth. At the same time, the Sugar Act also lowered the tax on sugar and molasses (a key ingredient in rum).

A year later, Parliament put into motion another tax. The Stamp Act required every piece of printed paper in the colonies to be **embossed** with a special stamp. Colonists would pay a fee to have marriage licenses, legal contracts, and other documents stamped. Books, newspapers, and even playing cards were included. The tax amounted to about one **shilling** per person each year. This was far less than the 25 shillings the average Englishman paid. Prime Minister George Grenville had proposed the Stamp Act. He felt that, surely, America would not object to such a small sum.

British officials used stamps such as these on goods sold in Britain and the United States. A stamp showed that the correct tax had been paid.

Colonists burned papers and other items bearing stamps to protest the Stamp Act.

But the colonists did object—and quite strongly. For one reason, the tax increase was a big one. It doubled the average American's yearly taxes.

More important, the Stamp Act was a direct tax on America. The colonists felt that Britain had no right to raise taxes within the colonies. Only their own assemblies should have the power to do that, they said. Yet what could be done? America wasn't allowed to send even one elected representative to Parliament to defend its rights. The colonies had no voice in their own fate. Boston lawyer James Otis declared, "Taxation without representation is **tyranny**!" The phrase would soon become a rallying cry across the land.

A REBELLIOUS CHILD

The colonies came together to protest what they considered unfair taxation. Together, they signed an agreement. They pledged not to buy any goods from Britain until the Stamp Act was **repealed.**

Groups of men called the Sons of Liberty formed in a number of American cities. In Boston, Massachusetts, the organization was led by a politician named Samuel Adams. The Sons of Liberty led public marches in support of the agreement. The group also pressured stamp masters to quit their jobs. (Stamp masters were in charge of distributing the stamps.)

At times, the Sons of Liberty turned to violence to achieve its goals. On August 26, 1765, an angry **mob** broke into the home of Thomas Hutchinson. Hutchinson was the lieutenant governor of Massachusetts Bay Colony. The rowdy group ruined every piece of furniture and china in the house. Hutchinson and his family barely escaped with their lives.

The destruction was caused by a rumor that the lieutenant governor had proposed the Stamp Act. Actually, Hutchinson opposed the tax. Yet he firmly believed all laws set down by Britain had to be obeyed. The colonists who felt the way Hutchinson did were known as **loyalists**. Those

BICKERING COLONIES

In the eighteenth century, the British colonies in America operated almost like separate countries. Each of the thirteen colonies had its own type of government, educational system, and cultural groups. The colonies did not trust one another. They were constantly arguing over control of territory.

Patriots led public marches to protest unfair taxation.

OUT FOR REVENGE

Anyone who got in the way of the patriot cause in New England might find himself tarred and feathered by a lawless mob. This nasty punishment involved pouring hot tar over the bare shoulders, chest, and back of the victim before covering him in a layer of feathers. It could take weeks for the tar to come off. When it finally peeled away, it usually took large strips of flesh with it, causing terrible pain. Many people died from the ordeal. Most of those who survived never fully recovered.

who supported the Sons of Liberty were called **patriots.** The two sides often clashed with words, fists, and, sometimes, weapons.

In the end, the colonies simply ignored the Stamp Act. King George was outraged. America was seen as a "rebellious child" who needed to be punished. Britain's new prime minister, William Pitt, had opposed taxing the colonies. But even he began to worry that Americans were carrying "their notions of liberty too far." In a speech before Parliament, Pitt said, "This is the mother country, they are the children; they must obey, and we prescribe."

British merchants were soon hurt by the loss of sales. In 1766, they pressured their government to repeal the Stamp Act. Yet, on the very same day the act was repealed, Parliament passed the Declaratory Act. This gave Britain the power to make decisions for the colonies "in all cases whatsoever." The colonies were too busy celebrating their triumph over the Stamp Act to be concerned about the new law. That would soon change.

TEA AND TRAGEDY

In 1767, Parliament hit the colonies with another set of taxes. These were known as the Townshend Acts. They were named for Charles Townshend (TOWNS-end), the British treasurer who proposed them. The Townshend Acts taxed all glass, paper, lead, and paint the colonies **imported** from Britain. It also charged three pennies per pound on all British tea. (Like most European countries, Britain did not grow its own tea. Instead, tea was imported from places like China and India).

The colonists were furious. Taxing British citizens for importing goods from their motherland was going too far. To protest the Townshend Acts, the colonies refused to import British tea. This was especially difficult because the colonies were bound by law to buy tea only from Britain.

British treasurer Charles Townshend proposed a new set of taxes in 1767.

Cutting back on tea wasn't easy. Everyone from laborers to society ladies enjoyed a few cups on a daily basis. Together, the colonies drank more than one million pounds of tea each year. A favorite blend was Bohea (BOE-hee), a rich, black tea that was named for the hills in southeastern China where it grew. Patriots needed a way to convince colonists to give up their favorite drink. So they claimed that Bohea tea was unhealthy for mind, body, and country. "Tea is really a slow poison, and has a corrosive [unhealthy] effect upon those who handle it," wrote Dr. Thomas Young. "I have left it off since it became a political poison, and have since gained in firmness of constitution. My substitute is chamomile flowers."

King George III wanted to make it clear to the colonies who was in charge. In the fall of 1768, he sent troops to Boston. Four thousand **redcoats** in a town of fewer than 17,000 people ignited a firestorm of anger. As tensions grew, fights broke out between soldiers and citizens.

INDEPENDENT WOMEN

To help protest the Townshend Acts, women throughout the colonies joined the Daughters of Liberty. They signed pledges not to drink British tea and encouraged merchants to stop selling it. At home, they experimented with herbs and flowers to create their own Liberty Teas. Raspberry leaves, peppermint, violet blossoms, and rose petals were just some of the plants that found their way into liberty teapots.

George III hoped to prove his authority to the colonists by sending troops to Boston in 1768.

This illustration shows Boston at about the same time George III sent British troops there. Shortly after the troops arrived, tensions heightened between colonists and soldiers.

Colonists didn't hesitate to express their dislike of British troops. Conflicts between the two groups would eventually become violent.

Edward Garrick was a young barber's apprentice. On the night of March 5, 1770, Garrick went to collect payment from a British officer at the customs house. The guard on duty would not let Garrick in. "Some angry words were interchanged between the sentinel [guard] and the boy," recalled George Hewes, a 28-year-old shoemaker who'd joined the crowd outside the customs house. People began taunting the guard. They dared him to shoot. A British officer, Captain Thomas Preston, and several other soldiers quickly arrived. They were not able to break up the group.

Paul Revere's engraving of the Boston Massacre was intended to inflame Bostonians against the British troops occupying their city.

Suddenly someone shouted, "Fire!" Thinking it was an order from his captain, a nervous soldier pulled the trigger. The shot caused other soldiers to fire their guns, too. When the thick clouds of white smoke cleared, three colonists lay dead. Two others were dying, and nine more were injured.

* * * *

The event was a tragic accident. Even so, Samuel Adams saw it as a chance to get the troops out of Boston. He began calling the incident "the Boston Massacre" to stir up public outcry against the British military. One of Adams's friends was a silversmith named Paul Revere. Revere created an engraving showing a line of redcoats gunning down citizens. This outraged the colonists. Most did not know the truth.

Soon, thousands of furious Bostonians gathered in Faneuil Hall, a meetinghouse in the city. They sent a committee to Thomas Hutchinson, now the governor of Massachusetts. The committee was led by Samuel Adams. Adams demanded that Hutchinson order the soldiers to leave Boston. At first, Hutchinson argued that he had power to move only one regiment. But when faced with the possibility of a massive uprising, the governor gave in. He sent both regiments to Castle William, an island in Boston Harbor.

As luck would have it, on the very day of the Boston Massacre, Parliament repealed the Townshend Acts. The tax was not bringing in enough money. Even so, Mother England did not intend to loosen her grip on her "rebellious child." As a symbol of Britain's power over its colonies, King George and Parliament let part of the Townshend Acts remain: the tea tax. It would be a few months before news of the Boston Massacre would reach Britain. The event was viewed as another sign that things in the colonies were getting out of hand.

THE PATRIOT VERSUS THE LOYALIST

For more than thirty years, Samuel Adams and Thomas Hutchinson would be bitter enemies. In 1764, while working as a tax collector, Adams had come up short on his collections. Hutchinson accused him of stealing the money. Actually, Adams was too kind to pressure those who couldn't pay. In turn, Adams complained that Britain appointed too many colonial officials. As a result, Hutchinson was removed from a special governor's panel.

17

This coat-of-arms belonged to the English East India Company.

DEUS INDICAT

DEO DUCENTE NIL NOCET

TROUBLE BREWING

In 1773, the English East India Company was in hot water. Although the colonies were bound by law to buy tea only from Britain, this London company constantly struggled to compete against Dutch tea being **smuggled** into America (and Britain, too). The colonies' agreement not to buy British tea had only added to the problem. Now, the company had more than seventeen million pounds of tea sitting unused in a London warehouse. It was facing financial ruin.

Something had to be done. So, Parliament came up with a plan. Originally, tea was shipped from China or India to merchants in England. The merchants would then reship the tea to America, raising the price to make a profit.

In May 1773, Parliament passed the Tea Act. This act gave the East India Company the right to sell tea in the colonies through its own **tea agents** in America. The three-cent-per-pound tax set down by the Townshend Acts would remain. But selling tea directly to the colonies would cut out the English middlemen—and their profits. The Tea Act meant the colonists could buy tea from the East India Company for half what they were paying for smuggled tea. British officials were certain the Americans would be so

Parliament passed the Tea Act in May 1773. British lawmakers hoped to help the financially struggling East India Company.

Colonists across the country were outraged once they learned about Parliament's passage of the Tea Act.

thrilled to save money they would forget all about their fight against unfair taxation.

To their surprise, the Tea Act sparked fury in America. A drop in the price of tea wasn't going to make people forget the unjust tax. Colonists were also worried that the new act would drive out competition in the marketplace. This would allow Britain to have more control over the colonies' economy. The full story of the Tea Act reached America in the fall of 1773. By then, seven ships carrying two thousand chests of tea from the East India Company were already making their way across the Atlantic Ocean. Four of the ships were bound for

In 1773, a fleet of seven ships carrying tea crossed the Atlantic Ocean. The ships and their cargo belonged to the East India Company.

★ ★ ★ ★

Boston. The other three were headed for ports in New York, Pennsylvania, and South Carolina.

Colonial leaders and the Sons of Liberty put pressure on royal tea agents. They wanted the agents to refuse to accept the tea. In Boston, messages were sent to Governor

Thomas Hutchinson remained firm in his decision to allow British tea ships to enter Boston's port.

*   *   *   *

Hutchinson asking that he turn the ships around when they reached port. But Hutchinson refused. He was determined to uphold all laws passed by Parliament.

The first of the ships, *Dartmouth*, sailed into Boston Harbor on Sunday, November 28, 1773. *Eleanor* arrived on December 2. It was followed five days later by the **brig** *Beaver*. (The fourth ship, *William*, got caught in a storm and ran aground off Cape Cod in Massachusetts.) The Sons of Liberty posted armed guards at Griffin's Wharf. They wanted to make sure not a single chest of tea was unloaded.

Meanwhile, Governor Hutchinson continued to insist that the ships would not be sent back to Britain. On December 8, he ordered that no ship would be allowed to leave Boston without a special permit. A flagship was moved to block the outgoing channel so that none of the tea ships could set sail.

THE FATHER OF AMERICAN INDEPENDENCE

Although he helped organize the Sons of Liberty, Samuel Adams did not approve of its use of violence. He preferred the pen to the sword. In his lifetime, Adams wrote thousands of letters to colonial leaders and newspapers to protest the way Britain treated its colonies. (He often used fake names to avoid punishment.) As a result of his efforts, he earned great respect from patriots such as Thomas Jefferson, John Hancock, and John Adams (Samuel's cousin).

Things couldn't stay this way for long. By law, the tea needed to be paid for within three weeks of its arrival. After that, it could be seized by customs agents and turned over to the royal tea agents for distribution. Samuel Adams knew that if the colonists drank even one drop of the tea they would be giving in to British taxes and trade policies. Their battle would be lost. Adams and his fellow patriots began crafting a plan to make sure that didn't happen.

By December 1773, patriots were gathering to discuss opposition to the Tea Act, as well as the fate of the tea ships docked at Boston harbor.

The Old South Meeting House dates back to 1729. It was the largest building in colonial Boston and was used for both religious services and public meetings.

A CALL TO ACTION

On December 16, 1773, a bone-chilling rain cast a gloomy spell over Boston. As evening approached, the skies began to clear. But the mood inside the Old South Meeting House was anything but calm. Several thousand people had gathered there. They wanted to hear the fate of the three ships docked at Griffin's Wharf.

The patriots tried once more to convince the governor to let the ships leave. They sent Francis Rotch, whose family owned the *Dartmouth*, to Hutchinson's home outside of

Boston. Rotch was supposed to have been back at Old South by three o'clock. But he had not yet returned by sunset. People were getting restless.

Finally, shortly before six o'clock, Rotch hurried into the hall and delivered the bad news: The governor had not changed his mind. Hutchinson knew time was on his side. In less than eight hours, at the stroke of midnight, the deadline for unloading the cargo would be up. Customs officials could then seize the tea. The crisis would be over.

Samuel Adams rose to his feet. "This meeting can do nothing more to save the country," he said. Immediately, a loud war whoop came from the gallery. Near the entrance of the

In the years leading up to the American Revolution, colonists gathered at the Old South Meeting House to challenge British rule.

hall, a group of colonists dressed as Mohawk Indians yelled and waved axes. People began shouting and cheering.

"The Mohawks are come!"

"Boston Harbor is a teapot tonight!"

"Who knows how tea will mingle with saltwater?" cried merchant John Rowe.

John Hancock declared, "Let every man do what is right in his own eyes!"

Colonists dressed as Indians dumped thousands of pounds of tea into the Boston harbor.

Townspeople poured out of Old South to join the Mohawks, who were leading the way to the wharf. George Hewes stopped at a nearby blacksmith shop. He covered his face and hands with coal dust and dressed "in the costume of an Indian, equipped with a small hatchet."

On the street, he fell into step with others wearing similar disguises: a blanket tied around the waist, a crooked feather in a cap, and red paint or soot smeared across the face. "We surely resembled devils from the bottomless pit rather than men," said sixteen-year-old Joshua Wyeth, a blacksmith.

As the procession neared the harbor, the whoops and whistles faded away. The time for talking had come and gone. Now it was time to strike a blow for liberty.

TEA OVERBOARD!

It was close to seven o'clock when the Mohawks arrived at Griffin's Wharf. Between 60 and 120 men assembled at the docks. The Mohawks were organized into three groups. They were not armed with guns or weapons. Following their

More than three hundred chests were split open and thrown into the harbor. A cheering crowd on the dock shouted its approval for the brewing of this "saltwater tea."

group leaders, the men quickly boarded *Dartmouth*, *Eleanor*, and *Beaver*. They ordered the customs agents to leave. The ships' crews were instructed to go below deck. Everyone did as they were told.

This tea chest was one of the two that survived the Boston Tea Party.

George Hewes was assigned to the brig *Beaver.* Once onboard, Hewes had orders to get the keys to the hatches and a dozen candles from Captain Nathan Coffin. "I made the demand accordingly, and the captain promptly replied, and delivered the articles; but requested me at the same time to do no damage to the ship or rigging," said Hewes. Coffin need not have worried. The Mohawks were not out to hurt anyone. Nor did they want to destroy anything other than what they had come for: 90,000 pounds (41,000 kilograms) of British tea.

"We then were ordered by our commander to open the hatches, and take out all the chests of tea and throw them overboard," said Hewes. Using slings, the patriots began lifting the chests of tea onto the decks.

Axes easily split into the thin wooden lids of the chests. It was much tougher cutting through the thick canvas sacks that held the loose tea. (All the tea sold in colonial times was loose; tea bags weren't invented until the twentieth century.) Once the tea was exposed, the chest was carried to the rail. The contents were thrown into the harbor, followed by the empty chest. Between them, the three ships carried 342 chests. Each chest held about 250 pounds (115 kg) of tea. Dumping all of it into the water was a long, difficult process. "I never worked harder in my life," said young Joshua Wyeth.

There was a low tide that evening. The water level beneath the ships was only about 3 feet (90 cm) deep. With so much

CAPTAIN'S LOG

"Between six and seven o'clock this evening, came down to the wharf a body of about one thousand people, among them were a number dressed and whooping like Indians. They came on board the ship, and after warning myself and the customs-house officers to get out of the way, they undid the hatches and went down the hold, where was eighty whole, and thirty-four half chests, of tea, which they hoisted upon deck, and cut the chests to pieces, and hove the tea off overboard, where it was damaged and lost."

—Captain James Hall

Dartmouth logbook, Thursday, December 16, 1773

All of the tea in the boxes was loose, and each box weighed approximately 250 pounds (115 kg).

tea going overboard, it soon began to pile up. Some of the men waded out into the water to push the black goop out into the harbor.

As the Mohawks worked, townspeople continued to gather along Griffin's Wharf. Yet, "entire silence prevailed—no clamor, no talking," said Robert Sessions. The only sound that echoed through the chilly autumn night was the sharp crack of wood breaking.

WHO WERE THE MOHAWKS?

Most of the colonists who dumped tea into Boston Harbor were tradesmen, such as carpenters, weavers, and merchants. In 1835, author Benjamin Thatcher made a list of fifty-eight men that participated in the Boston Tea Party. Fifty-five more names were added in the 1880s. George Hewes claimed that he tossed tea alongside John Hancock, but Hewes was probably mistaken. Patriots such as Hancock and Samuel Adams were so well-known that it was unlikely they would have joined in to dump the tea.

Most of the colonists involved in the Boston Tea Party were tradesmen, such as this woodworker.

The fact that many of the Mohawks were tradesmen, such as the shipbuilder shown here, probably made them better able to handle all the chopping and heavy lifting.

After all of the tea was dumped, the ships were cleaned and inspected to make sure there was no damage to the vessels.

MISSION ACCOMPLISHED

As the chests broke apart, some of the tea spilled onto the ships' decks. A few patriots couldn't resist grabbing handfuls of loose tea to take home. Those who were caught were tossed into the water, along with their stolen tea.

By nine o'clock, all of the tea onboard the ships was destroyed. "After having emptied the whole, the deck was swept clean, and everything put in its proper place," said Sessions. "An officer on board was requested to come up from the cabin and see that no damage was done except to the tea." Only a padlock was broken. It was replaced the next day. Before leaving, the patriots lined up on the dock

★ ★ ★ ★

Boston Harbor Tea is still sold today.

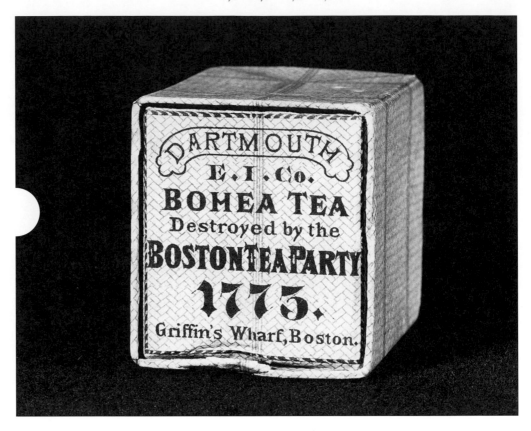

DARTMOUTH
E.I.Co.
BOHEA TEA
Destroyed by the
BOSTONTEAPARTY
1773.
Griffin's Wharf, Boston.

TASTE HISTORY FOR YOURSELF

The tea tossed into Boston Harbor came from Davison Newman and Company, Ltd., of London. Founded in 1650, the company is still in business today. You can even buy Boston Harbor Tea. It is the very same blend of tea that met a watery grave in 1773. Printed on the label is the petition sent by the company to King George III following the tea party. The company asked to be paid for the chests drowned by "persons disguised as Indians."

and took off their shoes. They emptied any remaining tea into the water.

The British troops stationed at Castle William knew what was going on at Griffin's Wharf. Even so, the redcoats did nothing to stop the event. "I could have easily prevented the Execution of this Plan," wrote British Navy Admiral John Montagu the following day, "but must have endangered the Lives of many innocent People by firing upon the Town." Nobody wanted another Boston Massacre.

Though many viewed the Boston Tea Party as a courageous act, the British still tried to punish the colonists for their actions, as this cartoon shows. The woman represents America. The British prime minister is pouring a pot of tea down her throat, and she is spitting it back at him.

Still, the Admiral felt a need to speak up. He raised the window and called out to a group of patriots. "Well, boys, you have had a fine, pleasant evening for your Indian caper, haven't you? But mind, you have got to pay the fiddler yet!"

"Oh, never mind! Never mind, squire! Just come out here, if you please, and we'll settle the bill in two minutes," challenged Lendall Pitts, a patriot military officer.

The admiral quickly shut the window.

A fife player among the patriots struck up a tune. The men marched on.

Their task complete, the Mohawks went their separate ways. When Hewes arrived home, he told his wife, Sally, everything that had happened.

Hutchinson and other British officials were determined to seek out and punish those involved in the Boston Tea Party.

"Well, George," she replied, inspecting his blanket and stained face. "Did you bring me home a lot of it?"

The honest shoemaker did not have a speck of tea on him.

A TURNING POINT

From Maine to Georgia, "the destruction of the tea" was viewed as a courageous act. When the tea ship *Polly* arrived in Philadelphia on December 26, it was sent back to England two days later. New Yorkers turned away a similar ship, *Nancy*. In Charleston, South Carolina, the tea was put into storage where it was left to rot.

Governor Hutchinson vowed to bring the criminals to justice, but no one was talking. The only person arrested for dumping tea was a barber named Eckley. He was later released because of lack of **evidence.** In fact, most people did not find out exactly who the Mohawks were until well after the American Revolution.

For more than sixty years, only George Hewes's family and close friends knew of his secret. In 1833, journalist James Hawkes discovered Hewes's identity. He asked the 91-year-old shoemaker to share his memories for a book. When Hawkes's book was published a year later, it brought Hewes into the national spotlight. He became a frequent guest at Independence Day festivities across the United States.

When news of the drowned tea made its way across the Atlantic Ocean, much of Britain was shocked. No one had expected such an act of rebellion. To punish the colonies,

A CLEVER NAME

For more than sixty years, people often referred to the raid on the tea ships as "the destruction of the tea." The term Boston Tea Party didn't appear until the mid-1830s. Historians don't know where the phrase came from, but it may have been a publisher's idea. It first appeared in books such as James Hawkes's *A Retrospect of the Boston Tea-Party with a Memoir of George R. T. Hewes* (1834) and *Traits of the Tea Party: Being a Memoir of George R. T. Hewes* (1835) by Benjamin Thatcher.

General Thomas Gage was a British general and governor of Massachusetts at the beginning of the American Revolution.

Parliament passed a series of laws in 1774. These became known in America as the Intolerable Acts. The laws shut down the port of Boston, and British troops were sent to occupy the city. The laws also stated that people could no longer hold town meetings or vote for officials. King George named General Thomas Gage, commander of the British forces in North America, the new governor of Massachusetts Bay Colony. (Thomas Hutchinson went to England and never returned to America.)

The king hoped to separate Massachusetts from the rest of the country, forcing the colony back into line. Instead, the Intolerable Acts had the opposite effect. The people of Hanover County, Virginia, expressed the feelings of many colonists. "If our sister Colony of Massachusetts Bay is enslaved, we cannot long remain free." American cities began sending food and supplies to Boston.

In September 1774, the First Continental Congress met in Philadelphia. Twelve of the thirteen colonies adopted a set of resolutions called the Declaration of Colonial Rights and Grievances. The document stated that all taxes set

down by Parliament took away the rights of the colonies. It also called for a repeal of the Intolerable Acts. Most patriots hoped that Parliament would come to understand their point of view. But it was not to be. A year and a half after the Boston Tea Party, the first shots of the American Revolution would be fired.

"The destruction of the tea is so bold, so daring, so firm, so intrepid, and inflexible," John Adams wrote in his journal, "and it must have so important consequences, and so lasting, that I cannot but consider it as an epoch [significant event] in history." Indeed, the Boston Tea Party had ignited a flame for liberty. It had also shown the colonies that they could stand together. America was ready to become a nation. It was ready to fight for the right to be free.

Glossary

allies—two or more persons or groups that have formed a connection to achieve a common goal

brig—a two-masted sailing vessel that is smaller than a ship

embossed—to have something imprinted with a stamp, leaving a raised design

evidence—information used to prove the guilt of someone accused of a crime

imported—goods brought in from another country

loyalist—a person who supports a ruler or government; in colonial America, a loyalist backed the laws set down by the British government

militia—an army made up of civilians who may undergo military training and serve full-time in emergencies

mob—a lawless or unruly group of people

Parliament—a nation's legislative body, often made up of elected and nonelected representatives

patriot—a person who firmly supports or defends their country

redcoats—in colonial times, British soldiers serving overseas

repealed—a law that is undone or revoked

shilling—a unit of currency

smuggled—brought into a country secretly, either because the goods are illegal or to avoid paying a tax on them

tax—a fee charged to citizens by their government to pay for running the country

tea agents—in colonial America, those who took delivery of imported tea and were responsible for its distribution

tyranny—the cruel and unjust use of power to rule over others

Timeline: The Boston

1763	1764	1765	1766	1767	1768

In North America, Britain and its colonial militia are victorious in the French and Indian War.

Parliament passes the Sugar Act.

Parliament approves the Stamp Act. The colonies protest by agreeing not to import British goods. In Boston, Samuel Adams organizes the Sons of Liberty.

Parliament repeals the Stamp Act and passes the Declaratory Act.

Parliament authorizes the Townshend Acts.

In the fall, 4,000 British troops are sent to Boston.

Tea Party

1770	1773	1774	1775	1776	1783

On March 5, five colonists are killed in the Boston Massacre. All of the Townshend Acts are repealed, except the tax on tea.

In May, Parliament passes the Tea Act.

· · · · · · · · ·

November 28: The first British tea ship, *Dartmouth,* weighs anchor in Boston; *Eleanor* and *Beaver* arrive within the week.

December 16: A group of patriots dressed as Mohawk Indians dump 342 chests of British tea into Boston Harbor.

Parliament enacts the Intolerable Acts. On September 6, the First Continental Congress meets in Philadelphia.

The American Revolution begins.

The colonies sign the Declaration of Independence to proclaim their freedom from British rule.

The United States wins the American Revolution and is acknowledged by Britain as an independent nation.

To Find Out More

BOOKS

Fritz, Jean. *Can't You Make Them Behave, King George?* New York: Putnam & Grosset Group, 1996.

Hakim, Joy. *From Colonies to Country (1710–1791): A History of US.* New York: Oxford University Press, 1999.

Stewart, Gail. *The American Revolution.* San Diego: Thomson Gale, 2004.

VIDEOS AND DVDS

The American Revolution. Vol. I, II, III, and IV, 1994, A & E Home Video. Videocassette.

Liberty! The American Revolution, 1997, PBS Home Video. DVD.

ONLINE SITES AND ORGANIZATIONS

The Boston Tea Party Ship and Museum
Congress Street Bridge
Boston, MA 02210
www.bostonteapartyship.com

"Liberty! The American Revolution"
The Public Broadcasting Service (PBS)
www.pbs.org/ktca/liberty

Index

Bold numbers indicate illustrations.

About the Author

A former television news reporter and weather forecaster, **Trudi Strain Trueit** is an award-winning journalist who has contributed news stories to ABC News, CBS News, and CNN. She has written more than twenty books for Scholastic on nature, wildlife, health, and history. Some of her books for Franklin Watts include *Storm Chasers, Clouds, Volcanoes, Keeping a Journal,* and *Dreams & Sleep* and for Children's Press her books include *Lizards, Snakes, Turtles,* and *Alligators and Crocodiles.*

Born and raised in the Pacific Northwest, Trudi has a bachelor's degree in broadcast journalism. She loves photography, painting, and reading (especially history). Trudi and her husband, Bill, a high-school teacher, make their home north of Seattle in Everett, Washington.